Discovering Chichester and District

The city walls and surrounding gardens of Chichester.
(Photo courtesy of T. Sellence)

David Harrison

S.B. Publications

By the same author
Exploring Eastbourne and the South Downs
Exploring Brighton and the South Downs
Exploring Ashdown Forest
The South Downs Way

First published in 2004 by S. B. Publications,
19 Grove Road, Seaford, East Sussex BN25 1TP

ISBN 1 85770 274 3

Designed and typeset by CGB, Lewes. Tel: 01273 476622
Printed by Fotolito Longo, Italy.

CONTENTS

ABOUT THE AUTHOR

David Harrison was born in Doncaster, Yorkshire in May 1943, son of a railwayman. A move to Kent in 1970 started his interest in rambling, with the North Downs Way and the Pilgrims' Way offering an ideal opportunity to explore the northern parts of that county. Business commitments in Cambridgeshire gave him the chance to walk much of East Anglia before making his home in Sussex in 1987. There his successful newsagent's business brought him into constant touch with visitors seeking advice on places of interest and walks in the area and, since his first book *Exploring Eastbourne and the South Downs* was published in 1995, subsequent projects have had him walking the South Downs on a regular basis. He is now retired – and still walking.

Front Cover: St Richards Walk leading to the precincts of Chichester Cathedral.
Back Cover: Arundel Castle.
(Front and back cover photos courtesy of T. Sellence).

INTRODUCTION

Chichester is unique. It has the only ancient cathedral visible from the sea. Its maritime situation played a vital role in its development by the Romans who established their principal port in the south at Dell Quay in Chichester Harbour. With the establishment of Londinium as a major stronghold it soon became necessary for a direct link to be made between the two cities for quick and easy transportation of goods and troops. Stane Street was the result, unique insomuch that it was the only road conceived, designed and built by the Romans with a specific purpose. All other Roman roads in Britain followed the path of ancient British trackways.

Arundel, too, is unique, for it is the only town in the country with a church shared by both Protestants and Roman Catholics. The parish church of St Nicholas is separated by a glass screen from Roman Catholic Fitzalan Chapel, built about 1380 and restored in 1886 by the fifteenth Duke of Norfolk.

The castle is impressive and there are other buildings worthy of note in the area. The Elizabethan mansion at Parham belonged to the same family for more than three centuries; at Bramber there is the magnificent medieval St Mary's where Queen Elizabeth I really did spend the night; at Uppark there is a lovely house with a dark past where that great writer on time and space, H G Wells, grew up.

The eight walks penetrate deep into the West Sussex countryside. They include full route directions, information on items of interest, and details of such practicalities as toilet and refreshment facilities. Where public transport is available, details of routes and times are given. These would have been correct at the time of going to press but do check before travelling.

DAVID HARRISON
SPRING **2004**

Bignor Hill, where Stane Street, the road the Romans built to link Londinium to
their principal port at Dell Quay, meets the South Downs Way.

CHICHESTER – A SHORT HISTORY

THE ROMANS

The Regni tribe, at their hill-top settlement at the Trundle, awaited the
Romans with some trepidation. When the tribune Vespasian finally landed
at Bosham Creek with the 2nd Legion in AD42, the Regni leader
Cogidubnus offered no resistance, greeting the Romans warmly. Although
he could not have known it at the time, his reaction to the situation was in
his best interest for later Vespasian was to become Emperor of Rome.

The Romans persuaded the Regni to leave their hilltop stronghold and
form an alliance in a new tribal capital at the head of the navigable part of
the creek. As a reward for his co-operation, Cogidubnus was honoured by
being appointed Imperial Legate. The Romans established a base camp on
the present site of Chichester, laid it out as a market town and
administrative centre with two main streets crossing at right angles, much
as it appears today, and called it *Noviomagus,* 'the new city of the plain'.

Around AD200 the city walls were built, originally mounds of earth
forming an eleven-sided polygon with gates at the end of each of the main
streets named after the cardinal points – Northgate, Southgate, Eastgate

and Westgate. The walls stretched for one and a half miles around the new town, enclosing an area of about 100 acres. Inside, there would have been an amphitheatre, forum, public baths, a temple of Neptune and Minerva and the governor's basilica.

The Anglo-Saxons
After the Romans left, the city fell into the hands of the Anglo-Saxons who

immediately strengthened the walls against the marauding Vikings. The Saxon chief Aella, who landed about AD477, gave the settlement to his son Cissa, calling the town Cissa's Caester (castle) from which its present name developed.

Christianity reached the area in AD681 when St Wilfrid, banished from the see of York, landed at Selsey and set up the diocese of the South Saxons. A church was built dedicated to St Peter, and this may well have been the predecessor to the present cathedral, for there is no trace today of any other Saxon church other than tiny St Olave's, pictured left, the oldest ecclesiastical building in the city.

The Normans
It was the Normans who appreciated the strategic value of Chichester, once more strengthening the walls and building a wooden castle within them, later reinforcing it with stone. Their greatest achievement, however, was the building of its cathedral. Ralph de Luffa, who became bishop in 1091, began the work which was not finished

until 1240. It has twice been damaged by fire and desecrated by the Puritans, but is still much as it was in the twelfth and thirteenth centuries, its graceful 277 foot spire visible for miles around. The separate bell tower was built in the fifteenth century and stands near the north porch.

The Middle Ages

Chichester's medieval farmers and merchants prospered. Wool was the main product of the surrounding area and a healthy export trade grew up. Later, cloth and wheat played an important part in the city's economy and the Market Cross, which dominates the city centre at the crossing of its two major highways, was the gift of Bishop Edward Story in 1501.

Much of the architecture of today's Chichester is Georgian, with some magnificent houses showing just how prosperous its merchants had become. The best way to see the city is from its Walls Walk. Then, having appreciated the panorama of its buildings from a distance, take to the streets and discover its wealth of architecture at close hand.

The south east quadrant entrance to the Wall Walks.

CHICHESTER WALLS WALK AND CITY WALK

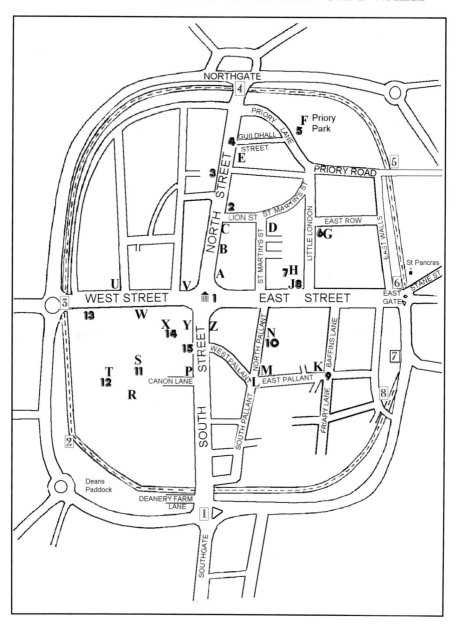

CHICHESTER WALLS WALK

1 Starting from SOUTHGATE, at the southern end of SOUTH STREET, follow the signs through DEANERY FARM LANE to the River Lavant footpath. This is **Dean's Paddock,** once part of the great defensive ditches, the spoil from which would have formed part of the original wall of which a bastion built in the fourth century can still be seen.

Dean's Paddock with an uninterrupted length of the citywall and a fourth century bastion.

2 Follow the footpath to the main road, turning right below the walls to Westgate. Here modern development has destroyed the sense of city enclosure, but on crossing the end of West Street and looking right, there are fine views of the Market Cross and Bell Tower. To the left, in Westgate, there are some splendid eighteenth century houses.

3 The Walk now continues along a wide, well-surfaced promenade with interesting roof-tops and house backs on the left and the enclosed city buildings to the right. The detached ruins of a bastion are visible over the wall to the left and at this point the rather architecturally-uninteresting West Sussex County Council offices dominate the view to the right.

4 Follow the signs across NORTH STREET, where NORTHGATE would have been, turning left on to the promenade with PRIORY PARK to the

The promenade passing Priory Park, given to the public by the Duke of Richmond in 1918.

right. Ahead, the eye-level roof-tops of the backs of the old cottages give a good impression of the height of the wall at this point. As the promenade swings round to the right, there is a good view across the city, with the mound of the wooden castle captured by the French in 1216 and destroyed by the English the following year. Nearby is the thirteenth century **Franciscan Friary,** later the **Guildhall**. The area to the left, beyond the Wall at this point, was once the Roman and then a medieval cemetery. It was totally destroyed by Parliamentarians in the Civil War.

5 Leave the wall by the lower gateway and cross PRIORY ROAD. Turn left to climb a broad flight of steps to gain access to EAST WALLS with a single-storey Art Nouveau style building to the left, beyond which is a school. Shippam's Edwardian style factory dominates the view to the right. The walk descends to EAST STREET where the East Gate stood – perhaps the most significant of the city's gates for it was from here STANE STREET began its long route to London.

6 Turn left into EAST STREET as far as the neo-Gothic church of **St Pancras,** at the start of STANE STREET, which in former times was lined by villas and farms on its way out of the city. A little way from here is an old graveyard in which Lady Frankland lies. She was a serving-maid who saved the life of Admiral Frankland in an earthquake and came to be remembered as Agnes in the story-poems of Oliver Wendell Holmes.

The section of the city wall from Eastgate continues down a private lane, disappearing and re-appearing behind and through buildings and gardens. To continue the Walls Walk, turn right at Eastgate Square, where, at No.11 John Keats stayed in January 1819 and began writing one of his best-known poems, *The Eve of St Agnes.* A plaque commemorating his stay can be seen high on the facing wall. Eastgate Chapel, the city's oldest Nonconformist place of worship, dates from 1671. One of its founders was George Smith, grandfather of the three Smith brothers who established their artistic reputations in London but returned to spend the rest of their lives in Chichester. Their father, William, was a minister of the chapel.

7 Walk past the Market on the left, where excavations have revealed life going back to Neolithic times. Beyond was the Roman amphitheatre but nothing of this remains today. Just visible behind trees on the right is the Greek-inspired Chapel of St John, designed by James Elmes and built in 1812 as a proprietary chapel, one with all the seating owned by those who had subscribed to its building.

8 Turn right at the Walls Walk signpost and into the car park. The Walk continues past the council buildings and along Theatre Lane where once stood a malthouse and granary which was used as a theatre from 1764 until 1850. After it closed theatrical performances and concerts were held in the Assembly Rooms. Turn right into SOUTH STREET to end the Walls Walk.

CHICHESTER CITY WALK

A further exploration of this fascinating city can be made within the outer walls, along the four main thoroughfares and through the Pallants – a

miniature replica of the main plan and using the map on page eight. The walk begins from the Market Cross, but may be joined at any point on the route.

1 Proceed along NORTH STREET where the **Butter Market (A)** is soon approached on the right. A little further along is the church of **St Olave (B)** and beyond that is the colonnaded **Council House (C).**

2 Turn right along LION STREET and then right again into ST MARTIN'S STREET where the curious old building of **St Mary's Hospital (D)** can be seen on the left. Go back to NORTH STREET and turn right.

3 Pass **31 North Stree**t with its fine, cantilevered first floor window above the premises of wine

Chichester Market Cross

and spirit merchant Arthur Purchase, to the **Ship Hotel (E).**

4 Turn right down GUILDHALL STREET and left into PRIORY PARK where the **Guildhall (F)** is situated.

5 Return to PRIORY LANE and follow the boundary of the park on the left as far as LITTLE LONDON, so called by Elizabeth I because she found it

so busy on her visit there. Turn right here and at its junction with EAST ROW is the **museum (G).**

6 Continue down LITTLE LONDON as far as the entrance to the car park on the right. Enter the car park and bear left to the church of **St Andrew, Oxmarket (H).**

7 Near its west door is a twitten or passageway leading through to EAST STREET and at this point the building on the right is **21 East Street (J).**

8 Turn left into EAST STREET, then right into BAFFINS LANE which has the colonnaded former Corn Exchange on the corner. At the junction of EAST PALLANT (right), NEW TOWN (left) and FRIARY LANE (ahead) is **Baffins Hall (K).**

9 Turn right into EAST PALLANT, where at the junction of the four **Pallants (L)** is **Pallant House (M).** A little further up NORTH PALLANT is **7 North Pallant (N).**

10 Return to the crossroads and turn right along WEST PALLANT, emerging at SOUTH STREET where turn left, then right, through **Canon Gate (P)** and along CANON LANE, with VICAR'S CLOSe to the right. A little further along the **Deanery (R)** is on the left.

11 **St Richard's Walk (S)** leads to the precincts of the cathedral, but continue ahead through PALACE GATe and into BISHOP'S PALACE GARDENS, with the **Bishop's Palace (T)** over to the right.

12 Either walk through the gardens or take the steep path upto the left onto the Wall promenade and follow it to WESTGATE and turn right along WEST STREET.

13 Westgate House is on the left, at the entrance to County Hall. **St Peter's Church (U)** then the **Army and Navy (V)** are two more buildings of architectural interest along WEST STREET before reaching the **Bell Tower (W)** and the **Cathedral (X)** on the right.

14 Leave the cathedral and turn right into the churchyard to **Vicar's Hall and Crypt (Y)**

15 Go under the little arch into SOUTH STREET where turn left past **69 South Street (Z)** back to the Market Cross.

POINTS OF INTEREST

(A) Butter Market

Built in 1807 to the design of John Nash, it replaced the Market Cross as

accommodation for small traders. An upper storey was added in to the building in 1900 for the Art Institute which was transferred there from its premises in Crane Street. It was here that carver, engraver and typographer Eric Gill (1882-1940) studied when his family moved to Chichester from Brighton in 1897.

(B) St Olave's Church

This church was here even before Bishop Ralph began to think about building his cathedral. It has been refashioned, but one of the original Saxon doorways is still in its walls and two Roman urns were found built into the wall above the east window, possibly containing the ashes of martyrs. The little church is only 40ft (12.2m) long and holds no more than seventy worshippers. It has a lovely sixteenth century chest with eight carved panels and there is a fourteenth century piscina with two little heads on the canopy. But even these seem young beside its Saxon arch and the Roman material in its walls.

(C) Council House

The Council Chamber and Assembly Rooms was built in 1731 to the design of Roger Morris. Lord Burlington had originally provided designs, at the request of the 2nd Duke of Richmond, but they proved too grandiose for the city council. The Neptune and Minerva Stone, which records the dedication of a Roman temple, is built into the wall of the Council

Chamber. It was found on the other side of Lion Street in 1723 and presented to the duke, who built a temple at Goodwood to house it. It was later returned to the city. Paganini and Liszt appeared in concert at the Assembly Rooms .

(D) St Mary's Hospital
Beneath the vast, high pitched roof of this twelfth century nunnery was a chapel and a hall which was used as an infirmary. In the eighteenth century the infirmary was divided into a number of small apartments to provide homes for the elderly and frail. Today its caring role and layout has changed little although the seven flats, each with its own bed-room and sitting room, now have mains services and all other amenities of modern living. In the  early days the hospital also catered for poor travellers, and they had to be genuinely poor. Those who feigned poverty and were found to have money in their pockets were severely flogged.

(E) Ship Hotel
This tall, red brick Georgian house on the corner of North Street and Guildhall Street was built around 1790 for Sir George Murray, one of Lord Nelson's admirals.

(F) Guildhall
Part of the former chapel of the Friary which occupied this site from 1269. When the Friary was dissolved in 1538, the building was granted to the mayor and citizens of Chichester and used as a Guildhall. It was here that William Blake, poet and painter, was tried for sedition at the county's Quarter Sessions in 1804. He was said to have uttered disparaging remarks, at the Fox Inn at Felpham, about the English reaction to Napoleon. Blake's friends, including Joseph Seagrave, the Chichester painter, and William

Hayley, the poet, made sure he had a good lawyer to defend him and the case was eventually dismissed.

The site of the Friary was excavated by Thomas King in 1835 and his finds were given to the Literary and Philosophical Society. Today the choir houses a branch of the Chichester District Museum and it is open on Saturdays between June and September.

(G) District Museum

Collections covering the geology, archaeology and social history of the Chichester district are housed in this eighteenth century former corn store. The sculpture symbolising 'discovery' in the forecourt is by John Skelton, nephew and last apprentice of Eric Gill. It was commissioned in 1963 by Stanley Roth.

(H) St Andrew, Oxmarket

Built in the thirteenth century above a Roman pavement, it is now the Chichester Centre of Arts. It is here that the eighteenth century poet, William Collins, was laid to rest in 1759. There is a memorial to him and his family inside. In the church there is a bust of William Cawley, who was one of the men to sign Charles Stuart's death warrant. At the Restoration he fled to Switzerland where he died in the year of the Great Plague. His body was brought back home and was buried in the chapel of St Mary's Hospital.

(J) 21 East Street

The present building was erected in 1927, on the site of the house in which William Collins, the poet, was born. His father was a hatter by trade and among his customers was Alexander Pope The premises were then occupied by a firm of printers for more than 150 years.

(K) Baffins Hall

Built in 1721 as a Presbyterian chapel.It became a Baptist chapel and then a Christadelphian chapel before becoming the auction house it is today.

(L) The Pallants

The four streets bearing the name Pallant are a miniature replica of the main city plan and are so called from the palings behind which red Sussex

Pallant House, built in the reign of Queen Anne, houses a collection of modern art.

cattle and Southdown sheep were penned for market. This was once a run-down area housing breweries, tanneries and squalid little cabins with thatched roofs.

(M) Pallant House

In 1712, during Queen Anne's reign, Henry Peckham, a young wine merchant who did so well out of port that he was called 'Lisbon' Peckham, built a red-brick mansion in North Pallant, with his crest of an ostrich on both gates. It was restored in the 1970s and contains a collection of modern paintings including those of Walter Hussey, Dean of Chichester from 1955-77. Here also are works by Graham Sutherland, Henry Moore, John Piper, Ivon Hitchens, Paul Nash and Ben Nicholson along with the world's largest single collection of Bow porcelain amassed by Geoffrey Freeman.

(N) 7 North Pallant

This house was the home of William Hayley, the poet, who sold it to John Marsh, the composer, who lived here until his death in 1828. In 1831 the

Literary and Philosophical Society bought the house, intending to build a museum and lecture room at the back. However they sold it four years later with none of the intended additions.

(P) Canon Gate
This sixteenth century gateway gives access to Canon Lane from which there is access to all the ecclesiastical premises of the diocese including the Vicar's Close, The Deanery, the Cathedral and the Bishop's Palace.

(R) The Deanery
Built in 1725 for Dean Thomas Sherlock to replace the original Deanery destroyed in the Civil War. W.F. Hook, Dean from 1859-75, came to Chichester from Leeds, where he had done tremendous reforming work. Anticipating a more peaceful time in Chichester, his plans went awry when, in 1861, the cathedral spire collapsed and he spent the remainder of his office fundraising for the rebuilding programme.

(S) St Richard's Walk
A stone-flagged path where a saint is said to have taken his exercise. The saint in question was Richard of Wych (1197-1253), the most celebrated Bishop of Chichester and the county's patron saint. When the Pope appointed him to the see in 1245, Henry III, who had appropriated its revenues, was so angry that he forbade anyone to even house or feed him. At first Richard was dependent on charity and on his friend Simon, parish priest of Tarring. To visit his flock he had to go round the entire county on foot. He was a stickler for clerical privilege and when the men of Lewes

dragged a thief out of sanctuary and hanged him, he made them cut down the rotting corpse and bury it in the sanctuary. He was much loved by the people and was canonised only a few years after his death. In 1273 his body was placed in a silver-gilt shrine in the retrochoir and pilgrims flocked to it, especially on his feast day, 3 April.

(T) Bishop's Palace
The episcopal palace, with its fine eighteenth century front, has a dining room with wooden ceiling adorned with painted coats-of-arms. It also has a thirteenth century chapel with one of the most precious gems of English art, the Chichester Roundel of the Madonna and Child, painted in delicate blue more than 700 years ago. It is believed to be the work of Matthew Paris who was writing his *Chronicles* in a monastery at St Albans the year after King John signed the Magna Carta.

(U) St Peter's Church
Built in 1852 the church is no longer used as a place of worship. It now houses an arcade of shops.

(V) Army & Navy Store
The former Oliver Whitby School for Boys, founded in 1702, closed in 1950 and has also been put to commercial use. However its crest can still be clearly seen above the main entrance to a famous department store.

(W) Bell Tower
This is the only campanile left at an English cathedral. The impressive structure, 120 feet high, with its charming turrets and a parapet, contains eight bells. One bell is older than the Spanish Armada and another weighs almost four tons.

(X) The Cathedral
A Saxon church dedicated to St Peter occupied this site when the Normans moved the bishopric to Chichester from Selsey in 1075. Ralph de Luffa, who became the bishop in 1091, began building the cathedral which was

not finished until 1240. It is similar in design to a cathedral in Normandy, which is hardly surprising as much of its stone came from Caen and the twin towers of the Abbaye-aux-Hommes at Caen are repeated here.

Chichester Cathedral and its Bell Tower.

After York Minster and St Paul's in London, this is the widest of all the cathedrals in England. It has two aisles on each side of the nave and three tiers of massive arches, almost 200 in all. They are a marvellous spectacle, with the great arch at the bottom, the double arch above and the triple arches reaching to the roof.

There are no early stained glass windows, indeed the best windows are quite modern, but there is quite a collection of unusual things to see and appreciate. Perhaps the most remarkable are the two great stones set in the wall of the south choir aisle. They are from the mother cathedral at Selsey, now lost beneath the sea. Each stone is about 6ft square and is superbly carved with figures, the features of which are full of feeling.

There are only two brasses here. One is to William Bradbridge and his wife Alice with their six sons and eight daughters, dating from the sixteenth century. The other is a nineteenth century brass to Dean Burgon. It is set in the floor under a fine thirteenth century triple canopy in the south transept. A white marble statue of William Huskisson, MP for Chichester, stands below the window dedicated to his memory. He was the first man killed on a railway. He went to see George Stephenson's engine, only to be run down by it.

The choir is more than 100ft long. It is rich in wood and the choir stalls are renowned for being some of the best work of fourteenth century craftsmen. The tomb to one side of the altar is that of Bishop Storey, the man responsible for building the Market Cross. Indeed, there is something here for everyone, be it works of art from almost every period; statues or monuments by great craftsmen such as John Flaxman, Henry Westmacott or Eric Gill; and wonderful chapels like the Lady Chapel, reached through gates of Sussex iron – the only ironwork in the cathedral.

(Y) Vicar's Hall and Crypt

After the cathedral, the Crypt is the oldest building in the city. It was already old when the Vicars' Hall was built over it in 1397. The clerics had separate houses in Vicars' Close in the fifteenth century and the Hall and its adjacent rooms were no longer needed for communal living. As late as 1598, the vicars, by now numbering four, were being admonished to dine there together once a week. The rooms were then let out to tenants and continued to be until the present century.

(Z) 69 South Street

Here Benjamin Martin lived between 1729-42, 'one of the most eminent mathematicians of the age', according to his obituary. Interested in all aspects of mathematics, he designed a number of microscopes, invented a weight-driven clock, improved magnetic compasses and wrote more than eighty books, including text books for students.

A Prospect of ARRVNDELL CAstle & Towne on y Weft fide

Arundel in 1644 with the parish church of St Nicholas on the left and the castle on its hilltop, before it was bombarded and captured by Cromwell's army. Below is an engraving by W Archer of the church and castle in 1842.

ARUNDEL – A SHORT HISTORY

Although not a large town, Arundel has always been one of importance. The Romans used it as a station when they constructed their road from Chichester to Pevensey and later Alfred the Great is believed to have built a stronghold here to defend the Arun valley against sea raiders. It remained a royal town until the reign of Harold Godwinson, the last king of Saxon England, and there has been a castle here since Edward the Confessor.

After the Norman Conquest Roger de Montgomerie, Earl of Shrewsbury, was granted the earldom of Arundel and he rebuilt the castle in the early 1070s and raised the status of the busy little port on the tidal River Arun to that of a borough. The earldom came into the Fitzalan family by marriage in the thirteenth century and Edmund Fitzalan became the 8th Earl in 1302.

Arundel was traditionally named after *Hirondelle* (the swallow), the name of the horse of the giant Bevis of Southampton, who was warder of the gatehouse of Arundel Castle in Norman times. A swallow is the crest on the coat-of-arms granted to the town in 1939.

In the Domesday survey of 1086 Arundel appears as:

CASTRV HARVNDEL, T.R.E.[*tempore regis Edwardi*] reddeb de qda. molino. XL folid. de. III.

conuuiis. XX. folid. de uno paftico. XX. folid . . .

which, being translated, reads:

ARUNDEL CASTLE before 1066 paid 40s from a mill; 20s for three banquets; and 20s for one entertainment . . .

When the male line of the Fitzalans died out in 1580, Arundel was inherited by Philip Howard, Earl of Surrey, son of the Duke of Norfolk and a Fitzalan heiress and a member of the leading Roman Catholic family in the land. The head of their family, the Duke of Norfolk, holds the oldest and most important hereditary title in Britain. He is Earl Marshal of England and it is he who is responsible for all major state occasions.

His devotion to the Church of Rome, in the reign of the Protestant Queen Elizabeth I, cost Philip Howard, 13th Earl of Arundel, his life. A letter from him to Cardinal Allen in France asking how best he could serve the Catholic faith was intercepted by Sir Francis Walsingham, the queen's spymaster, who sent him a fictitious reply advising him to flee to the continent, which he did. He was arrested on a ship at sea, for it was an offence to leave the country without the permission of the monarch, and was imprisoned in the Tower in 1585.

Four years later he was tried for treason, accused of following the Catholic faith and praying for the success of the Spanish Armada. He was found guilty and sentenced to death, but Elizabeth chose not to sign his death warrant. He was not informed that this was so and spent the next six years in the Tower thinking each day might be his last. He petitioned the queen to be allowed to see his wife – and the son he had never met. Elizabeth replied that if he would attend just one Protestant service she would free him and restore all his properties and power but he would not accept the offer. After ten years imprisonment in the Tower he contracted dysentery and died without ever seeing his son. In 1970 Philip Howard was canonised by Pope Paul VI and is now the patron saint of the diocese of Arundel and Brighton.

Arundel Castle was based on Windsor Castle with a central motte between two baileys. It was badly damaged during the Civil War when it was seized by Cromwell's Roundheads, commanded by Sir William Waller. After a siege lasting about three weeks it was captured and left roofless and in a sorry state of repair for more than a century.

It was partially restored in 1718 but the old Norman keep on the motte remained a ruin and was used as an aviary for a time. There was further restoration towards the end of the eighteenth century but the castle, in its present form, is the creation of Henry, 15th Duke of Norfolk, who succeeded in 1860 when only thirteen. He inherited vast wealth, with estates all over

Arundel Castle today, with the ruins of the Maison Dieu in the foreground.

England, and rebuilt Arundel with fine taste, retaining as much of the original building as he could, including the imposing Norman keep. The square embattled barbican towers, with a portcullis doorway and a wooden drawbridge, are splendid examples of the ancient defences – little changed on the outside but restored within. The modern towers still show traces of ancient masonry but almost everything inside, although in the style of the thirteenth century, is the work of the 15th Duke.

The town itself is best explored on foot. The Town Walk starts from the High Street with its fine mixture of building styles. It goes along the old port, which played such an important part in Arundel's medieval history, before rising to the ecclesiastical area and the ancient church of St Nicholas and the more modern cathedral. The walk returns to the High Street or, alternatively, includes a stroll through the castle's park, passing the Hiorne Tower, Swanbourne Lake and the Wildfowl Trust.

ARUNDEL TOWN WALK

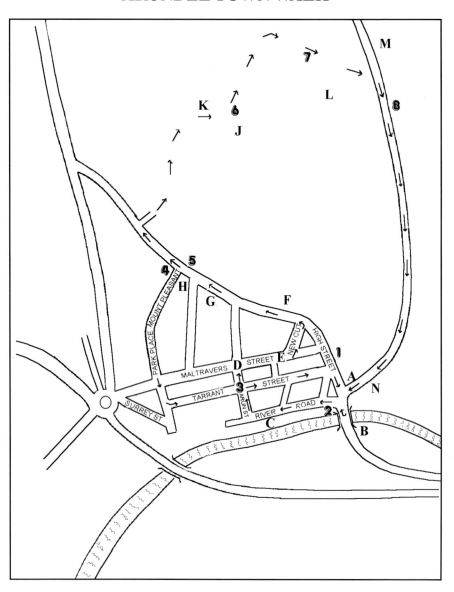

ARUNDEL TOWN WALK

1 From the Norfolk Arms, pictured above, a cheerful late eighteenth century red brick building, continue down past the **Square (A)** to the bridge crossing the **River Arun (B)**

2 Pass Town Quay, which leads into **River Road (C)**, turning right into ARUN STREET with its delightful collection of flint cottages on the left.

3 Continue up **Kings Arms Hill (D)** and turn right into MALTRAVERS STREET **(E)**. Turn left up NEW CUT to the parish **Church of St Nicholas (F)**. The **Cathedral of Our Lady and St Philip Howard (G)** stands a little further on the left, beyond which is **St Mary's Gate Inn (H)**

4 To return to the HIGH STREET, turn left down MOUNT PLEASANT, which soon becomes PARK PLACE, and turn left into TARRANT STREET at the junction with SURREY STREET. This will lead into the HIGH STREET opposite the Norfolk Arms.

5 To visit **Arundel Park (J)** continue on from St Mary's Gate Inn on the opposite side of the road and alongside the high wall. Follow this round right, keeping to the metalled road which eventually enters the park through the gateway. Keep to the road as far as the **Hiorne Tower (K)**

The Hiorne Tower, called after the architect,
Francis Hiorne, who designed it.

6 Turn right across the green below the tower and across the gallops in the direction of the yellow waymarker. Turn left over the stile, where there is a glorious view over the valley, and follow the track down to the cross-tracks, then turn sharp right back through the bottom of the valley.

7 Cross the stile keeping to the left of **Swanbourne Lake (L),** eventually passing the cafe and emerging at the road. To visit the **Wildfowl and Wetlands Trust (M)** turn left for 400 yards (360m).

8 To return to Arundel, cross the road and turn right along the pathway. At the river, turn left to follow the riverside walk or turn right and over the bridge to continue along the pathway. Both routes converge at **Maison Dieu (N),** where turn right into the HIGH STREET to end the walk.

POINTS OF INTEREST

(A) The Square
This area of the town was once full of medieval buildings with no water supply or sanitation. One of the residents, Edward Hamper, had a well which he agreed to lease to the town for a peppercorn rent so that the poor had a pure source of water. By 1773 all the buildings had become derelict and were pulled down, leaving an open Square with Hamper's well in the middle of it.

The cattle market was moved to the Square and in 1834 the town was

28

given a pump to raise the water from the well – a system that operated satisfactorily until well into the twentieth century. In 1921, by which time the town had a mains water supply, a memorial to those who fell in the First World War was raised on the site of the no-longer-needed well.

In 1974, the year of Local Government Reorganisation, the area was paved and surrounded with flower beds to mark the ending of Arundel's 900 years as a borough. A plaque recording this change of administrative status can be seen on the wall in front of one of the flower beds on the south side of the Square.

(B) River Arun

The current in this river is said to be the second fastest of any waterway in England. In medieval times a causeway led across the marshy valley through which it flows so swiftly into Arundel. The first stone bridge was built in 1724 to replace a timber one and the present bridge was constructed on the same site in 1935. Arundel was a busy port in the nineteenth century but the expansion of Littlehampton Harbour seriously affected its trade and the arrival of the railway made matters worse. When a permanent railway bridge was built across the Arun at Ford in 1935 tall ships could no longer reach Arundel and the town's days as a port were finshed.

(C) River Road

This road runs parallel to the river and was once bustling with trade and activity. Most of the old buildings have been replaced by private houses but some still remain.

There were more than thirty inns and alehouses in the once-busy port and Ship and Lighter

The Cathedral of Our Lady and St Philip Howard and, below, is the said-to-be 'smallest house in Arundel'.

Cottages was one of them. The antiques market on the opposite side of the road was formerly a warehouse for salt, and small ships were built at the Nineveh Shipyard as long ago as the sixteenth century. It later became a timber yard, then a wire works, before houses were built on the site in 1996.

(D) Kings Arms Hill

There is a good view of the cathedral from here and on the corner of Parson's Hill opposite is a terrace of handsome brick and stone gable roofed houses, Nos 40-44, designed by Joseph Aloysius Hansom, the Victorian architect and inventor of the Hansom cab. There is a statue of St Henry in a stone recess at first floor level on the south west corner of the block. He was crowned Holy Roman Emperor in 1014 and did much to consolidate the power of the Germanic monarchy and reform and reorganise the church. The reason for his presence in effigy is that he was the patron saint of the 15th Duke of Norfolk, who employed Hansom to design the new cathedral.

(E) Maltravers Street

A little way along the street divides into two levels with the buildings on the upper parade providing a far more interesting contrast in styles. On the lower level is the crooked timbered cottage on the corner of Bakers Arms Hill which was once promoted as the the 'Smallest House in Arundel'. It is one of the few in which the original beams can be seen from the outside.

The sombre flint building is the Town Hall where the council meets once a month and justice is dispensed by the magistrates once a week. The land for this building was given to the town in 1836 by the 12th Duke because he wanted to enclose the house behind St Nicholas church, where town meetings were then held, within the castle grounds.

(F) Parish Church of St Nicholas

This is arguably the finest building in Arundel. Certainly it is the most unique for it is the only church in the land shared by the Church of England and the Church of Rome. Records show that a church dedicated to St

31

The Fitzalan Chapel.

Nicholas existed prior to Domesday Book but nothing remains of the original, the present building dating back to 1380. There were no pews or seats in those days and unless worshippers brought their own seating they were obliged to stand throughout the service. A stone seat of a sort ran round the walls of the church, and the old and infirm made good use of it, giving rise to the saying 'the weakest go to the wall'.

During the Civil War the Roundheads used the church as a barracks and the Fitzalan Chapel as stables. They bombarded the castle with canon fired from the top of the tower.

With the restoration of the monarchy in 1660 the church once again became an exclusively Protestant place of worship. All was well until 1873 when the 15th Duke of Norfolk bricked off the Fitzalan Chapel from the nave, which the vicar claimed was part of the parish church. The High Court, in 1879, ruled that the chapel belonged to the Roman Catholic Duke of Norfolk. Hence the unusual situation of having two churches of different denominations under the same roof. The brick wall was demolished and a glass screen erected in its place in 1969, thus providing a superb view of the chapel from behind the reredos, access to which can be made from the castle grounds (fee payable).

(G) Cathedral of Our Lady and St Philip Howard

Originally known as the Church of St Philip Neri, it was commissioned by the 15th Duke of Norfolk soon after he came of age in 1868 and opened on 1 July 1873. It was designed in the French Gothic style by Joseph Hansom, who also designed Birmingham Town Hall and St John's Cathedral, Norwich. It was intended to be the parish church for the Roman Catholics of Arundel but was created a cathedral in 1965 and changed its dedication following St Philip Howard's canonisation in 1970. His remains have since been transferred from the Fitzalan Chapel to a newly built shrine, adorned by his coat-of-arms, within the cathedral. This striking tribute is possibly the finest feature of an otherwise drab building, best viewed from the outside and from afar.

(H) St Mary's Gate Inn

This was originally built in 1527 and has always been licensed to sell alcohol. It has been considerably altered over the years and what is now the main bar was an extension built to house the stonemasons working on the cathedral next door.

(J) Arundel Park

The park stretches north for more than two miles and covers an area of 1,200 acres. It was created by the 11th Duke of Norfolk in 1789 and its trees are predominantly beech, although its layout is constantly being changed and improved.

(K) Hiorne Tower

A splendid triangular, eighteenth century Gothic prospect tower, with attractive chequered flintwork walls, built in 1787, but in the style of the fourteenth century. It is named after its architect, Francis Hiorne, who the

11th Duke had in mind to design some of the rebuilding of the castle. Unfortunately this never happened as Hiorne died unexpectedly. Just in front of the tower is a Greek altar – a plinth brought back from the Crimean War by Lord Lyons.

(L) Swanbourne Lake
The main feature of Arundel Park is naturally fed by water draining down from the surrounding South Downs. Swanbourne Lodge was built in 1852 in the Jacobean style to the design of William Burn using knapped flint.

(M) Wildfowl and Wetlands Trust
When it opened in November 1976 this was the seventh national reserve of its kind in the country. It occupies some fifty acres of landscaped meadowland and reed beds which attract thousands of wildfowl, including sandpipers, snipe, kingfishers and reed buntings. Spacious observation hides allow the birds to be observed at close quarters and in the reception centre building there is a large viewing gallery, a lecture and film theatre, a restaurant, and a gift and book shop. The Trust is open daily throughout the year, with the exception of Christmas Day. There is an admission charge.

(N) Maison Dieu
Founded in 1396 by Richard Fitzalan, 4th Earl of Arundel, as a hospice for the care of the aged. It was originally part of a chantry college served by secular canons and consisted of a quadrangle containing a chapel, refectory and chambers. It was dissolved by Henry VIII and the lands given to the Earl of Arundel. In 1724 much of the hospice was pulled down and the stone used to build a new bridge across the River Arun.

EIGHT WALKS IN WEST SUSSEX

Walk 1 – Graffham

This is a walk which never fails to interest, whatever the season of the year. Beginning with the glorious views over the paddocks of Lavington Stud to the backdrop of the wooded South Downs, the route leads into Seaford College where the old blends in so perfectly with the modern. Then along a leafy lane before turning off to the Downs on the only steep uphill section of the walk. However, the view from Duncton Down Viewpoint is well worth the effort and from it the white house of Burton Park is clearly visible. A steady descent now, through Manor Farm to the Cricketers Arms and then into Burton Park with its interesting little church beside the white house. Duncton church may be visited by making a slight detour from the main route, which passes through Ridlington Farm and then on to Westerlands Stud before entering the woods, which are carpeted with bluebells in the spring and still very pleasant any other time of the year. The final stretch passes through Lavington Stud before returning to the church to conclude the walk.

INFORMATION BOARD

ACCESS/PARKING: By the church at the end of the village, west of the A285

MAP REFERENCE: Landranger 197, grid reference 929167

DISTANCE: 9 miles (14.4km)

TIME TO ALLOW: 3.5 hours

TERRAIN: Mainly level ground apart from a short, steep ascent of the South Downs and a steady descent into Duncton

TOILETS/REFRESHMENTS: Foresters Arms, Graffham and the Cricketers Arms, Duncton

ROUTE: Graffham–Lavington Stud–Seaford College–Duncton Down Viewpoint–Manor Farm–Cricketers Arms–Burton Park–Duncton– Ridlington Farm–Westerlands Stud– Graffham

---

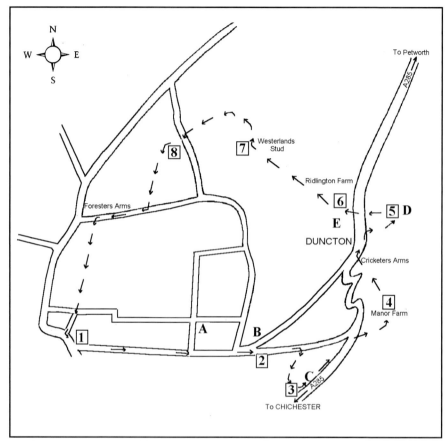

A – LAVINGTON STUD. **B** – SEAFORD COLLEGE. **C** – DUNCTON DOWN VIEWPOINT.
D – BURTON CHURCH. **E** – DUNCTON CHURCH.

Directions:

1 Follow the road south from Graffham past the church and turn left towards Seaford College. Continue along the road past **Lavington Stud (A)** to **Seaford College (B).**

2 Where the road swings off left by the imposing railings and gateway, keep right in the direction of the yellow waymarker, turning left along an attractive metalled lane. Turn right by Willow Cottage, then right again

**The restored thirteenth century church at Graffham from where the walk
starts – and ends.**

in the direction of the yellow waymarker, following the path up and round
left as indicated.

3 Within sight and sound of the A285 take the left fork, turning right at
the public footpath signpost as the path ahead descends rapidly. Enter
the car park at **Duncton Down Viewpoint (C)**. Return to the T-junction,
turn right down the steep descent to the road, and cross straight over into
Manor Farm.

4 Follow the yellow waymarkers round the farm to the road, where turn
right to the Cricketers Arms. Continue along A285, ignoring the
bridleway, and turn right into Burton Park and follow the path to **Burton
Church (D).**

5 Keep straight ahead out of the church, crossing a triangular green before
going over a stile and along a path leading to the chapel by the road. To
visit **Duncton Church (E)** turn left here and return. Cross straight over the
road, taking the narrow path between Downsview and the old Post House.

6 Cross the stile, taking the path to the left. Over another stile, crossing
the next field diagonally right to another stile beside a metal gate. Keep

ahead now along a good track to Ridlington Farm. From here follow all signs ahead to Westerlands Stud, which skirt round to the right.

7 Opposite the estate office turn right into the woods, turning left at the first signpost, then left again at the T-junction. Continue through the woods as far as the bridge over the stream. Cross the bridge and continue left beside the stream, in the same direction as before, as far as the road, where turn left, then right in 50 yards (47m), then left again at the next cross-tracks.

8 Keep ahead across a small paddock and into woods, then ahead across the next field to a cross-track, where turn right. Immediately before the war memorial turn left through a kissing gate and across a field in the obvious direction. For the Foresters Arms turn right at the war memorial and return. Keep ahead now until the spire of Graffham church guides you home.

POINTS OF INTEREST

(A) Lavington Stud
There are five studs on the estate that belongs to Lord Woolavington and the paddocks extend for miles. Westerlands Stud farmhouse (see point **6** of the walk) is the original home farm of the estate and the beams on the walls and ceiling of the fourteenth century house are the envy of many. The covered-in exercise yard of the stud is one of only a few in England, and it has been the home of a handful of world famous stallions, including Coronach and Hurry On.

(B) Seaford College
The college was founded in Seaford in 1884 to train boys for careers in the army, navy, the professions or commerce. It moved first to Worthing and, in 1946, to its present enviable location in 320 acres of wooded parkland at the foot of the South Downs. Many members of staff live in the park, helping to produce a community atmosphere. Girls were accepted, first into the sixth form from 1993, and now throughout the entire school.

(C) Duncton Down Viewpoint
At 398ft (121m) above sea level the view from this point is remarkable. The route already undertaken on the walk can clearly be seen at the foot of

Burton Park, home of John Sewell Courtauld, MP for Chichester from 1924 until his death in 1942. There is a memorial to him in Burton Church.

the Downs and Burton Park, with its sparkling white paintwork, is easily spotted. Midhurst can be seen over to the west and Petworth and its deer park is clearly visible to the north.

(D) Burton Church

The church, one of the smallest in Sussex, was built in 1075 and altered a number of times over the centuries. Its dedication is unknown – it is referred to simply as the parish church of Burton. Records of 1819 state that 'no service had been performed in the church for many years', but it is in regular use today.

The fifteenth century screen dividing the nave from the chancel retains traces of coloured decoration and the tiny rood loft, about 2ft wide, still survives. Against the south wall of the chancel, in a recessed tomb, is an effigy of a woman in a low-cut, close-fitting dress. She may well have been a member of the Dawtrey family who owned Burton around 1480, the date on the tomb. Against the north wall of the nave is an altar tomb beneath a canopy, richly carved of Purbeck marble, within which is buried Sir William Goring, who died 1553, and his wife, Elizabeth. There is no effigy of Sir William on the tomb but there is one of his wife, surprisingly shown wearing an heraldic tabard. It is the only sixteenth century effigy in England of a woman clad in an essentially male garment.

There are two wall paintings of note. On the eastern splay of the north window is a remarkable sixteenth century painting of a young, round-faced female figure with a mass of deep red hair, tied head downwards to a St Andrew cross. Over the south doorway is a large painting of the Stuart Royal Arms, dated 1636.

(E) Duncton church

Holy Trinity church was built by Lord Leconfield in 1866 to replace the much older St Mary's which had become derelict and been pulled down. Although it is structurally in the relatively modern Anglican Decorated style, with a pointed chancel arch and a tower with a small spire, it has a bell dated 1389. This is possibly one of the oldest church bells in the county and its origin has puzzled experts as the inscription on it indicates that it is Norman although from its appearance it was for a long time believed to be Dutch.

This unusual signpost shows St Christopher, the patron saint of travellers, pointing the way to the village of Harting.

Walk 2 – The four churches

A simple walk yet full of surprises. It begins at the restored church at Elsted, which is south-west of Midhurst, and follows a good path across open countryside to New House Farm with panoramic views across the western plains of Sussex. Soon the little church at Didling is reached, and with it comes the first surprise of the walk. The pleasant approach to Treyford passes the colourful signpost of St Christopher, through Manor Farm to the hidden remains of Treyford church and surprise number two. Further along the road is the village cemetery, where a third surprise reveals the fourth church. From here the return back to Elsted is only a short way across the fields along an obvious track.

INFORMATION BOARD	
ACCESS/PARKING:	Limited parking by the church at Elsted. Alternative parking at the Village Hall opposite the Three Horseshoes, Elsted
MAP REFERENCE:	Landranger 197, grid reference 816198
DISTANCE:	6 miles (10km)
TIME TO ALLOW:	3 hours
TERRAIN:	Over reasonably good paths across rural countryside, along metalled roads and obvious tracks. Fairly flat throughout.
TOILETS/REFRESHMENTS:	The Three Horseshoes, Elsted
ROUTE:	Elsted–New House Farm–Didling–Treyford (St Christopher)–Manor Farm–Ruined Church–Cemetery–Elsted

WALK 2 – THE FOUR CHURCHES

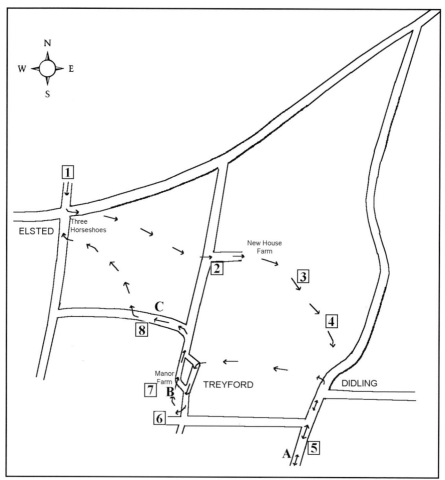

A – ST ANDREW'S CHURCH, DIDLING. B – ST MARY'S, TREYFORD. C – CEMETERY

Directions:

1 From Elsted church retrace route to the crossroads. Turn left past the
   Three Horseshoes immediately taking the public footpath up right, over
the stile and down left across the next field, following the obvious route to
the road.

2 Continue ahead along the wide track to New House Farm. Pass through three metal gates at the farmyard, keeping to the right of the farmhouse. At the third gate bear diagonally left to a stile in the corner of the next field, continuing along the edge of the field.

3 Go over the stiles, cutting off the corner of the field and continue ahead across the next field. Over another stile before following the hedge on the right, turning right at the corner and heading towards the long barn ahead.

4 Through a metal gate and over two plank bridges and continue over the brow of the hill to another stile, where turn right towards the buildings of Didling. The path gives way to a metalled lane by the Old Cottage. Turn right at the road and follow it to the church of **St Andrews, Didling (A).**

5 Retrace steps, turning left at the farm, and follow the signposted route into the woods and across the stream. Continue along the grass track between two buildings to the road where turn left, and at the St Christopher signpost, turn right.

6 Follow the path round right (ignoring the turning to the left) beside a high wooden fence. As the path bends back left continue ahead over the stile, following the hedge on the right. Turn right at the end of the hedge, crossing the stiles to continue through Manor Farm farmyard.

7 At the road, double back to visit the ruins of **Treyford church (B).** Continue up the road, turning left, which is signposted Elsted. On the right is the entrance to the **cemetery (C).**

8 Continue along the road to turn right opposite Treyford Cottage. Cross the stile by the public footpath to continue across the next field, following the obvious and well signposted route to the road. Turn right here into Elsted, crossing straight over at the crossroads back to the church.

POINTS OF INTEREST

(A) St Andrew's Church, Didling

The early names of Dedlinges and Dudelinges confirm that this place was once the territory of a Saxon tribal group known as the Dyddelingas or Dyddel's people. Around 1260 the name was shortened to Didelinge but it kept its two 'e's well into the Tudor period when it took on its present

St Andrew's, Didling with its nearly-lost yew tree and, below, the battered flint walls that al that is left of St Mary's, Treyford.

name. St Andrew – the Shepherds' Church – is both minute and charming and thankfully has escaped the restorers. With its smoke-blackened benches dating from the fifteenth century and its crude Laudian Communion rail from the seventeenth fencing off the Holy Table, this piece of antiquity is still lit by candles held in iron holders at the end of each pew.

Outside in the churchyard is a yew tree, as old and as big as the church itself. One day it was decided to lop the branches to prevent them damaging the decaying fabric of the church, but somehow the instructions were misunderstood. Fortunately the vicar arrived on the scene just in time to stop the workmen from cutting down the tree altogether. Careful inspection of the trunk will show how close the tree came to being felled.

(B) St Mary, Treyford
This is a sad and neglected place, difficult to find and yet right on top of the only road through the village. The church built here in the thirteenth century served the community well. It stood on a prehistoric mound that was once an ancient burial ground but now it is in ruins, the gravestones in its churchyard, some carved with cherubs, leaning isolated and untended among trees and undergrowth.

(C) Cemetery
A new church was built in Treyford in 1849 but a century later this one also fell into decay and the village was left with two churches, neither of which was suitable for worship. As falling masonry from the new church was creating a safety hazard it was blown up in 1951. Now all that remains of it is the outline of the foundations at the far end of the cemetery. St Paul's church at Elsted has since been sympathetically restored, and now serves the combined communities.

WALK 3 – APULDRAM

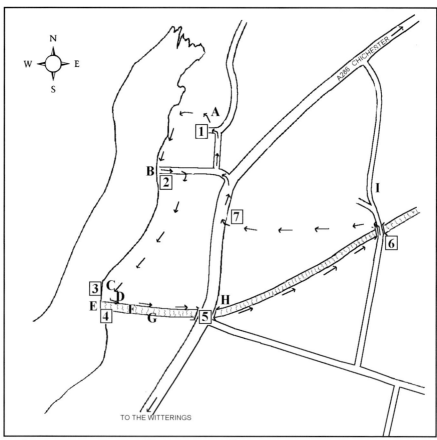

A – APULDRAM CHURCH. B – DELL QUAY. C – SALTERNS COPSE. D – CHICHESTER YACHT BASIN. E – SALTERNS LOCK. F – CHICHESTER CANAL. G – MANHOOD END LOCK. H – CUTFIELD BRIDGE. I –DONNINGTON.

Walk 3 – Apuldram

A fascinating walk into the past. The opening section skirts the backwaters of Chichester Harbour, visiting Dell Quay which was the main port in Roman times. The past is soon overtaken by the present on passing over the lock into Chichester Yacht Basin, but not for long, for ahead is the start of

Chichester Canal and the beginning of a remarkable piece of transport history. The walk leaves the canal at Donnington to return across arable land and the main artery of Manhood to Apuldram and its church by the Manor House.

```
┌─────────────────────────────────────────────────────────────────────────┐
│                          INFORMATION BOARD                                │
│ ACCESS/PARKING: At Apuldram church car park, south of Chichester          │
│ MAP REFERENCE: Landranger 197, grid reference 842033                      │
│ DISTANCE:        7 miles (11.2km)                                         │
│ TIME TO ALLOW: 2.5 hours                                                  │
│ TERRAIN:         Along good paths and tracks, with some short sections of │
│                  metalled road and along the edges of two fields. Flat    │
│                  surfaces all the way.                                     │
│ TOILETS/REFRESHMENTS: Crown and Anchor, Dell Quay.                        │
│ ROUTE:           Apuldram church–Dell Quay–Salterns Copse–Chichester      │
│                  Yacht Basin–Chichester Canal–Donnington–Apuldram church  │
└─────────────────────────────────────────────────────────────────────────┘
```

Directions:

1 Ahead to the church **(A)**. Follow the path to the left – or to the right if coming out of the church – to the coastal path, and then turn left to **Dell Quay (B).**

2 Follow the metalled road as far as Apuldram Cottage which is at the end of the row of houses. Turn right by the public footpath signpost and keep ahead to **Salterns Copse (C).**

3 The route through the copse leads to **Chichester Yacht Basin (D)**. Cross the lock (as permitted) and turn right at the T-junction to **Salterns Lock (E)** and the start of the **Chichester Canal (F).**

4 From Salterns Lock retrace steps beside the canal, passing the new Egremont Bridge, the site of the old Castor Bridge, and the disused **Manhood End Lock (G)**. Keep ahead by the canal along a broad green sward as the road slopes off left to the A286.

5 Cross the road and canal at **Cutfield Bridge (H)** to continue along the path with the now well-weeded canal on the left. Pass the remains of Dudley Bridge – the rails for its swing mechanism are still visible – to the road.

6 At the road turn left over the canal. To visit **Donnington (I)** keep ahead. To continue the walk, turn sharp left over the stile beside the entrance to

Old Manor House. Keep ahead as the drive turns off right, across the next field and follow an obvious route across a rough field. Cross over two plank bridges and go along the edge of the next field to the road.

7 Turn right at the A286, then left at the sign to Dell Quay and Apuldram.

Turn right in 200 yards (190m), then left at the sign to the church, to get back to the car park.

POINTS OF INTEREST

(A) Apuldram church

The name of the village has changed several times over the centuries from the Old English *apuldor hamm*, apple tree meadow. Even today church and state cannot make up their minds, the former favouring Apuldram, the latter Appledram.

The church was built around 1250 and has been little altered. The font is original and made of Purbeck marble, and the fine massive wooden screen dates from the fourteenth century. The farmhouse by the church, Rymans, has still the remains of a 45ft high tower built of the same stone as that of Chichester cathedral tower. The house was, it is said, intended to be a castle but Ryman could not get permission to fortify it so he handed over his materials to the builders of the cathedral.

(B) Dell Quay

Here was Chichester's port from Roman times until 1824 when the canal was cut and cargoes could be brought by barge straight to the city centre. During the reign of Elizabeth I it was described as being the best haven between Portsmouth and the Thames and provided a ship and fifty men to fight against the Spanish Armada in 1588. However, its navigable channel began to deteriorate so much that 10-tonners had difficulty making passage where once 40 ton vessels used to sail with ease. Cargoes then had to be transferred into barges for onward shipment and with the advent of the canal and the railways the port of Dell Quay was no longer commercially viable. Since 1945 it has become a flourishing centre for pleasure boating and has its own sailing club.

Dell Quay, once a Roman harbour now a yachtsman's paradise.

(C) Salterns Copse

Seven hundred years ago much of the present adjacent farmland would have been like this copse, dominated by huge oak trees interspersed with ash, birch, hazel, hawthorn and holly. It is managed today by Chichester Harbour Conservancy on behalf of Apuldram Manor Farm.

(D) Chichester Yacht Basin

The stretch of foreshore now converted into the yacht basin was once known as the Salterns and was a centre of the industry for getting salt from the sea. Salt was an essential commodity for the preservation of meat and fish before the days of refrigeration and the Domesday Survey lists 285 salt pans on the Sussex coast, the Salterns at Apuldram among them. Before 1287, when a great storm damaged many of the salt pans beyond recovery, Sussex was exporting salt to both Holland and France.

With the industry in decline what had once been exported now had to be imported. In the seventeenth century legislation was enacted to protect salt

49

In the summer today there are more waterlilies than vessels in passage in Salterns Lock.

working in the North Country, and this virtually finished off the Sussex salt industry. Only Apuldram survived until the mid-nineteenth century, when free trade agreements gave the market to imported salt.

(E) Salterns Lock

The lock, which measures some 100ft by 20ft, is still completely intact and operational. It is built of brick and was designed to accept vessels of up to 100 tons on their way to and from Portsmouth Harbour. On the south side of the canal is the Egremont Arms, an inn built to serve the barge traffic. It is now a private house.

(F) Chichester Canal

A short cut from Hunston, leading into Chichester, exists to this day. It was part of the Portsmouth and Arundel Canal project and designed by John Rennie (1761-1821). The section from the harbour to Chichester itself was constructed as a ship canal, permitting passage for vessels up to 85ft in length with a beam of 18ft. Traffic never reached the levels forecast and this section of the canal closed to commercial traffic in 1906, sixteen years short of its centenary.

(G) Manhood End Lock
Now disused and dismantled, this was the second of only six locks on the Portsmouth and Arundel Canal. Both lock gates have now gone, but the fabric of the lock is still good, although showing signs of decay. A concrete drain at the eastern end regulates both the water level back to Chichester and the outflow to Chichester Harbour.

(H) Cutfield Bridge
The A286 crosses the canal at Cutfield Bridge, a swing bridge named after William Cutfield of Climping, members of whose family were shareholders in the canal company. It was built by C and H Tickell of Southampton in 1820 and remained in use well into the twentieth century. The canal was eventually blocked around 1924/5 and was used as an anti-tank obstacle during the Second World War when the road bridges were raised and pill boxes defended the main road from the coast.

(I) Donnington
The thirteenth century church, at the end of a rough lane to the north of the village, has some traces of ancient glass in its windows and a replica font that has been remodelled on an earlier version with some of the original worked into the replacement. The church, which was damaged by fire in 1939, was used by nineteenth century smugglers as a store for their contraband cargoes.

On the road through the village is the schoolhouse,and the Old Manor House stands to the north of the remains of the Chichester Canal.

WALK 4 – ITCHENOR

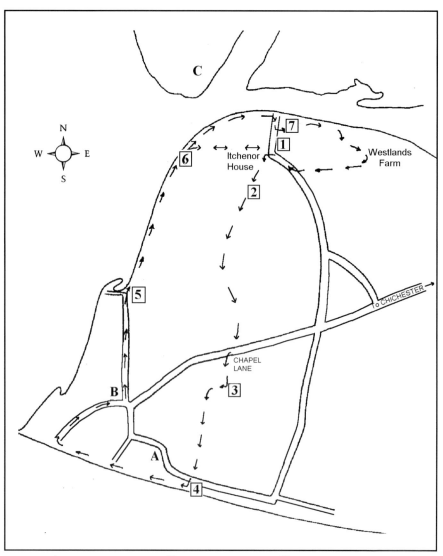

C

N
W — E
S

6

Itchenor
House

7

1

Westlands
Farm

2

To CHICHESTER

5

CHAPEL
LANE

3

B

A

4

A – CAKEHAM MANOR. B – WEST WITTERING. C – THORNEY ISLAND.

Walk 4 – Itchenor

This is a walk round the headland of the Witterings with much of its mileage either along the coast or around Chichester Harbour. From the stretch along the Channel there are glorious views past the entrance to Portsmouth Harbour and up Spithead to Southampton. The Isle of Wight stands proud in the distance and there is plenty of shipping to see.

From West Wittering a path leads to the coastal path round Chichester Harbour, passing some fine properties as it wends its way towards West Itchenor. This was one of the first areas to be colonised by the invading Saxons. The church, founded as a chapel in the twelfth century, is unusual, inasmuch that it has no structural division between the nave and chancel. During the Napoleonic Wars there was a large dock and shipyard at West Itchenor which made it a place of some importance.

The choice has to be made here whether to continue with the full walk or take the short cut back to the church. The short route skirts Itchenor House, while the full walk offers good views of Thorney Island, Chidham and Bosham on the way to West Itchenor with its busy harbour. The walk doubles back at Westlands Farm, crossing the fields to the road leading back to the church.

INFORMATION BOARD

ACCESS/PARKING: Limited parking by Itchenor church, south-west of Chichester

MAP REFERENCE: Landranger 197 grid reference 799006

DISTANCE: Full walk 11.5 miles (18.3km).
Walk A 10 miles (16km).
Walk B 3 miles (4.8km)

TIME TO ALLOW: Full Walk 5 hours. Walk A 3.5 hours. Walk B 1.5 hours

TERRAIN: Good paths through woods, across fields and along coast.
Footpaths and metalled roads in parts, all of which are fairly level and not too strenuous

TOILETS/REFRESHMENTS: West Wittering car park (Full walk and Walk A).
The Ship, West Itchenor (Full Walk and Walk B).

ROUTE: Itchenor church–Methodist chapel–beach–West Wittering car park–West Wittering–Rookwood–Coastal Path–West Itchenor–Westlands Farm–Itchenor church

---

Directions:

1 Carry on along the road from the church and ahead to Itchenor House. Turn left at the public footpath signpost immediately through the gates, crossing the farm track and continuing ahead across the next field. WALK B continues along the drive to Itchenor House, following the signs to the coastal path, where continue the walk from point **6**.

2 Keep ahead as the track swings off right and at the metalled road turn right, then in 50 yards (45m), left into Chapel Lane. Pass the Methodist chapel on the right before turning right at the public footpath signpost opposite Acre Street.

3 Keep ahead towards the farm buildings, turning left at the T-junction as far as the road. Turn right here, then left at the signpost by the corrugated metal gates. When the path reaches an open field follow the edge left to the road and cross straight over, continuing along Jolliffe Road. The castellated tower with flag aloft is **Cakeham Manor (A).**

4 At the seafront turn right, keeping ahead until turning right into the car park at West Wittering. Follow the road to the church **(B)** continuing along Ella Nore Lane to the coastal path.

5 Pass through the gate and turn right. At the signpost by the squeeze stile is where **WALK A** returns to the church via Itchenor House. The route is obvious and well signposted back to the church.

6 Continue ahead (**WALK B** turns right here) with good views across the harbour to **Thorney Island (C)**, Chidham and Bosham. Pass the boatyard to the harbour office, turning right into the village, then left opposite the Ship Inn.

7 Follow the coastal path, turning left opposite South Corrie along a metalled road. Turn right at the public footpath signpost and sharp right by Westlands Farm along a path to the right of a hedge. At the road, turn right to get back to the church.

POINTS OF INTEREST

(A) Cakeham Manor

This five hundred year-old house was originally built as a summer retreat for the Bishop of Chichester. Today it is owned by Eve and Ted Branson, parents of Richard Branson, and this patriotic couple never fail to have the Union flag proudly flying from its ramparts.

(B) West Wittering

This village at the western end of the Selsey peninsula could boast, at the time of writing, that it had more resident celebrities than any other in Sussex. Roger Waters, keyboard player with Pink Floyd, has sought solitude here, as has Michael Ball since achieving success with Andrew Lloyd Webber's music. Jonathan Morris chose to live in the village since finding fame in the long-running comedy success *Bread*, and Nicholas Lyndhurst, Rodney in *Only Fools and Horses*, has lived here since his early childhood.

The parish church of St Peter and St Paul is mainly thirteenth century with splendid arches and a Saxon font from an earlier church. On the chancel wall is a memorial to the men of the parish who perished in the First World War. It is an example of the early work of typographer and sculptor Eric Gill, whose father was vicar here from 1914 to 1930. The

West Wittering in the 1930s before the harbour was developed and the village became a haven for stars of stage and screen.

55

altar rails date from 1560 but the gates are modern. Older still is the wooden staircase which gives access to the belfry, known to date from 1250. The three bells housed in the belfry were hoisted to their housing by the winch now at the foot of the tower. It is a rare specimen and may well be the oldest winch in the country.

(C)Thorney Island

Thorney Island has been joined to the mainland for more than 100 years. The Royal Air Force arrived there in 1935 and its airfield went on to play an important part as a Second World War fighter station and as a base for Coastal Command. It was operational until 1976 when, after a brief period as a temporary home for the Vietnamese Boat People, it was taken over by the Army and is now the home base of a regiment of artillery. A public footpath follows the 7 mile (11.3km) coastal path round the island, most of which passes through Ministry of Defence property and so it is important to keep to the waymarked path to avoid trespassing. The church of St Nicholas in the village of West Thorney, only accessible via the coastal path, has one of the oldest inscribed bells in the country.

The ruins of Boxgrove Priory.

Walk 5 – Eartham

An interesting walk with a definite connection with the past. The outward route includes two sections through woodland before reaching the village of Boxgrove with its magnificent church and adjoining priory ruins. A short distance away is the hamlet of Halnaker, with the ruins of the once famous Halnaker House. Another short section gives access to Warehead Farm and the start of a delightful piece of Stane Street. On the way a path leads off to the windmill on Halnaker Hill from where the views are astounding. The walk then descends to Selhurst Park before turning off back to Eartham where, in the church, is a large plaque recording the death

---

INFORMATION BOARD

ACCESS/PARKING: By the church in the village of Eartham, north of the A27

MAP REFERENCE: Landranger 197, grid reference 938095

DISTANCE: 7 miles (11.3km)
Halnaker House ruins – plus another 0.5 mile (0.8km)
Halnaker Windmill – plus another 0.5 mile (0.8km)

TIME TO ALLOW: 3 hours for complete walk

TERRAIN: Reasonably level ground with the exception of Halnaker Hill and the final section from the A285 back to Eartham

TOILETS/REFRESHMENTS: Anglesey Arms, Halnaker or the George, Eartham

ROUTE: Eartham–Long Down–Boxgrove–Halnaker–Halnaker House (ruins)–Warehead Farm–Stane Street–Halnaker windmill–Selhurst Park–Eartham.

WALK 5 – EARTHAM

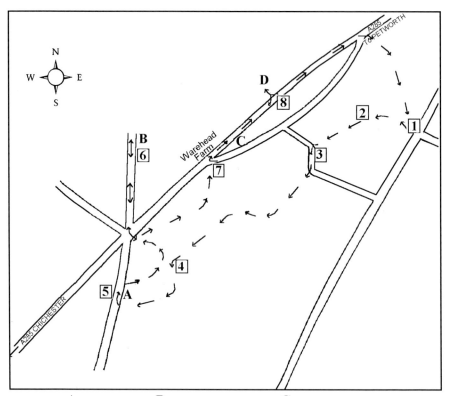

A – BOXGROVE. **B** –HALNAKER HOUSE. **C** – STANE STREET.
D – HALNAKER WINDMILL.

of William Huskisson, MP for Liverpool, the first man to be killed on a railway. He was at the formal opening of the Liverpool to Manchester line and, when the train carrying the official party stopped for water, the passengers descended to stretch their legs. The MP was crossing the track to speak to the Duke of Wellington when he fell down in front of the train and the engine ran right over him. George Stephenson picked Huskisson up and drove him on the engine to Eccles where, on the night of 15 September 1830, he died. Also remembered in Eartham church is Sir John Millbanke who won the Victoria Cross in South Africa.

Directions:

1 Leave Eartham by the public footpath beside the Old Vicarage opposite the church. Pass through the metal kissing gate, then fork diagonally left across the next field, heading towards the copse on top of the hill.

2 Cross the stile and keep to the left of the copse, maintaining the same alignment across the next field. Over another stile into the woods, bearing right downhill, then left at the public footpath signpost. Pass through the metal kissing gate to the road.

3 Turn left along the road and as it swings off left turn right at the public bridleway signpost. Cross straight over at the first track, turning right at the gravel road under the power lines. Keep ahead as the road narrows to a track into the woods. Where the track turns off right, keep ahead at the public footpath signpost, beside an avenue of young trees. The spire of Chichester cathedral can be seen way ahead in the distance.

4 Turn left at the T-junction, where there are good views of Boxgrove Priory to the right. In a short while follow the path round right to **Boxgrove church (A).**

5 Turn right through the village and right again immediately after the priory. Turn left at the T-junction following the path as it swings round left to a point where the path splits. Bear right here, but to visit Halnaker House ruins, keep left. Cross the A285 with care before forking right at Park Lane. Continue ahead along a gravel bridleway as the metalled road turns right into **Halnaker House**, the ruins of which are now ahead **(B).**

6 Retrace steps to the A285 which recross, returning to the public footpath signpost, where turn left to rejoin the main route. At the metalled road turn right, then in 100 yards (95m) turn left over the stile following a well signposted route across private land. Here sightings of deer are common.

7 Recross the A285 at Warehead Farm, turning right along a gravel track. Keep to the right of Mill Cottage and along **Stane Street (C).** The route rises rapidly now over Halnaker Hill and an obvious path gives access to **Halnaker Windmill (D)** at its summit.

8 Stane Street and the main route continues at this point up four steps and along a ridge. Go over a peculiar iron staircase stile before starting the descent of Halnaker Hill to rejoin the A285 by Seabeach House. Keep ahead past the entrance to Selhurst Park, before turning right at the public footpath signpost, and follow the obvious route to the metal kissing gate and back to Eartham.

POINTS OF INTEREST

(A) Boxgrove

This unassuming little village, which takes its name from an ancient grove of box-trees, achieved world recognition in 1993 with the discovery of a bone in a gravel pit. It proved to be the oldest human remain ever found in Europe, dating back over half a million years.

Of a much later date is the village's other claim to distinction. Boxgrove Priory, a Benedictine house, was founded in 1117 by Robert de Haye as a cell of the Norman abbey of Lessay. Only a few Norman arches and the roof-less guest house survive from the monastic buildings, but the thirteenth century nave and chancel and the magnificent chantry chapel, built in 1526, now form the present church of SS Mary and Blaise.

(B) Halnaker House

This was built by Thomas West, later Lord de la Warr, around the remains of a medieval house and thirteenth century chapel. Halnaker House passed down through the centuries to the Countess of Derby, who built the almshouses at Boxgrove, and to the Duke of Richmond, who abandoned it once his new mansion at Goodwood was complete. It fell into ruin in 1800 and has since been left to the elements. A new Halnaker House was built by Lutyens in 1938.

(C) Stane Street

Built in the early years of Roman occupation of hammered chalk and flints and topped with a flint and gravel surface. It became one of the most important commercial highways in the south east, linking London with Chichester. Along it would have passed corn from the Downs, iron from the Weald and other goods from the continent. Only the raised central embankment or agger remains today.

(D) Halnaker Windmill

Built for the Duke of Richmond as the feudal mill for the Goodwood estates, where the tenant farmers were able to have their corn harvest ground into wheatmeal for their own use.

Records show there was a mill here as far back as 1540 although when the present one was built is not known.

It was struck by lightning in 1905 and the wooden windshaft was split and the cap damaged. The owners were not prepared to repair it and for a time it remained derelict. It was given new sweeps and fitted with an iron windshaft in 1956 and now qualifies as the oldest tower mill in Sussex.

WALK 6 – FITTLEWORTH

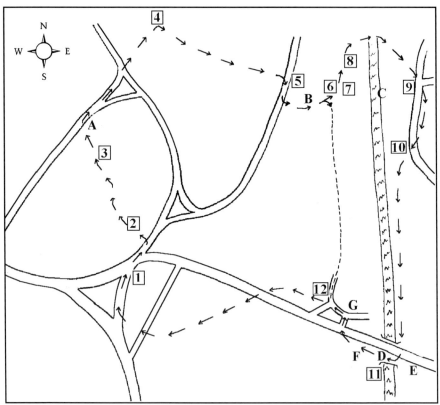

A –CROWSOLE. **B** – BRINKWELLS. **C**–CANAL. **D** –STOPHAM BRIDGE. **E** – WHITE HART.
F – STOPHAM HOUSE.. **G** – CHURCH OF THE BLESSED VIRGIN, STOPHAM.
Shortened version of walk indicated by ▬ ▬ ▬ ▬ ▬ ▬ ▬ ▬ ▬

Walk 6 – Fittleworth

A lovely walk, particularly in springtime when the bluebells are out. Little
Bognor, with its old flour mill, is picturesque and the woods beyond
Brinkwells, the one-time home of Sir Edward Elgar, are a delight. Here the
decision has to be made whether to continue with the full walk or opt for
the shortened version. The full walk continues on to Pallingham Quay Farm
where the remains of the canal which formed part of the Arun-Wey
navigation run adjacent to the infant River Arun. A part of the walk leads

down to Stopham Bridge and the welcome watering hole of the White Hart, before continuing to the twelfth century church at Stopham. The shortened version rejoins the main walk here. The final section skirts an old sand quarry before making the return to Fittleworth and its church.

INFORMATION BOARD

ACCESS/PARKING: By Fittleworth church, off the A 283

MAP REFERENCE: Landranger 197, grid reference 009193

DISTANCE: 10 miles (16km).5 miles (8km) shortened version

TIME TO ALLOW: 3.5 hours for complete walk.Three hours for shortened version

TERRAIN: Easy walking across fields, through woods and along metalled roads

TOILETS/REFRESHMENTS: White Hart public house, Stopham Bridge.None on shortened walk

ROUTE: Fittleworth church–Little Bognor–-Brinkwells–Pallingham Quay Farm–Stopham Bridge–-Stopham church–Fittleworth church.

Directions:

1 With the church behind, you set off right to A283, which cross with care and beware of the nasty bend. Turn down right, signposted Bedham, then left at the public footpath signpost beside Park Lodge. Cross the stile at the end of the first field, following the public footpath signpost to a second stile in the corner of next field.

2 Keep ahead through a small copse before crossing the next field along an obvious path. Follow the yellow waymarkers right, then left, then right again, keeping to the edge of the field. This section may be overgrown in the summer. Climb over a stile before passing through a leafy walk with a stream on one side and an orchard on the other.

3 Cross the stream before continuing by the hedge on the right, passing behind Dyers Cottage. Carry on along the gravel track to the road, where turn right into Little Bognor and past **Crowsole (A).** Take the left fork where the road splits, crossing straight over at the public footpath signpost past four huge sandstone boulders.

4 At the next cross-tracks, by a yellow waymarker, turn right along a narrow path into the woods. Climb over the stile and go along edge of next field then into more woods before emerging onto a wider track. Keep ahead by a low wall as the main track swings off to the right, then at the T-junction turn left to the road.

5 Turn right at the road, then left after 150 yards (140m) at the public footpath signpost to **Brinkwells (B).** Keep ahead over the stile, continuing along a path through woodland, finally crossing a stile on to the drive to Spring Farm.

6 Keep ahead as the drive turns left into the farmyard, following an obvious path to another stile at some cross-tracks. For the shortened version of the walk turn right here, keeping to the bridleway (blue way marker) through the woods. Keep ahead as the bridleway turns off right, then after 50 yards (45m), turn off left through a gate and across the field towards the South Downs. Continue ahead at the metalled road to the **church at Stopham (G)** to rejoin the main route. (See 11).

7 To continue with the main walk keep straight ahead at the cross-tracks, through the gate and turn left at the T-junction. Pass Lane End Cottage, where the views to the right are spectacular, then turn right over the stile at the public footpath signpost, keeping ahead along a narrow path which soon leads to another stile.

8 Keep to the left of the huge field, crossing the gallops and keeping ahead at the next field to Pallingham Quay Farmhouse. Keep ahead over the brick and concrete bridges over the infant Arun, before crossing the hump back bridge over the **old canal (C).** Follow the path round to the right before passing to the right of a corrugated iron farm building and keeping ahead at metalled road. Turn left at T-junction then right at the road by Pickhurst Farm.

9 Pass the road junction off left, then at the top of the hill, where horses cross, bear left over the stile and follow the gravel track which soon leads into a metalled track. Keep straight on to the right of a high hedge, crossing a stile to the road as the track swings off left. Follow the road up the hill and past some cottages, turning right at the public bridleway as the road swings off to the left.

10 Turn right where signposted, then left into the woods, once past the new

property on right. Follow the obvious track to the A283, which cross at **Stopham Bridge (D)** and the **White Hart (E)**.

11 Continue across the old bridge past **Stopham House (F)**, turning right at the signpost to Stopham to the **Church of St Mary the Virgin (G)**. Continue past the church, taking the first turning left, then keeping straight ahead at Coronation Cottages as the road swings off left. Here the shortened version of the walk joins the main route.

12 Keep ahead at the public footpath signpost as the bridleway swings off to the right, following the footpath to the road. Cross straight over and keep ahead by the backs of the houses, ignoring all paths off to the left. Cross straight over the road and at the B2138 turn right into the Church of St Mary the Virgin, Fittleworth and back to the car park.

POINTS OF INTEREST

(A) Crowsole
A twelfth century overshot flour mill which ceased working in 1895 and is now a private house in a pretty setting.

(B) Brinkwells
Sir Edward Elgar came to live here in May 1917, when he was suffering from depression brought on by the First World War. His wife, Alice, found the house and fell in love with it. Elgar himself was no less enthusiastic, telling a friend: 'It is divine. A simple thatched cottage and soiled studio with a wonderful view . . .' Two years here worked wonders for his health and his music. It was at Brinkwells he wrote both his great 'cello concerto and his piano quintet. Today the house is still unspoilt, unmodernised and much as he left it in the same lonely setting, carpeted in spring with primroses, bluebells and wood anemones.

(C) Wey and Arun Canal
Here was part of the Arun-Wey Navigation, the only navigable waterway connecting the Thames with the south coast. The River Arun was navigable from the sea to just south of Pallingham. The Arun Navigation Company, founded in 1785, built the canal to make the river navigable as far as

Stopham Bridge.

Newbridge, where work stopped in 1793 because of a financial crisis caused by the Napoleonic Wars. The navigation could not compete with the faster and more efficient railway system and closed on 1 January 1888.

(D) Stopham Bridge

Built around 1309 and rebuilt in 1403. Six of the arches are original but the seventh, in the centre, was raised in July 1822 to permit the passage of barges as part of the Arun-Wey Navigation. It is now preserved and open only to foot traffic.

(E) White Hart

The building dates back to the thirteenth century and has been an inn since 1500. Before there was a police force, England was dependent on the militia to maintain law and order. Each county was allocated a manpower quota for this purpose and if it failed to reach its target it was fined. Some 500 men from the Royal Lancashire Militia were recruited for duties in Sussex and made their way south to Chichester. On arrival they were told they would have to march to the barracks at Horsham before they could collect their bounty money. On the 23 August 1807 a party of disgruntled militia-men, on their way from Chichester, stopped off at the White Hart for rest and refreshment. Because the innkeeper failed to serve them quickly enough they helped themselves to his stock and a full scale battle ensued, with many casualties. Today service is a little quicker and the clientele less aggressive.

(F) Stopham House

The home of the Barttelots, a family which has been in Sussex since the Norman Conquest. Once they were able to ride from Stopham to Horsham without ever leaving their own lands and it was a Barttelot who built the medieval bridge. The surname was recorded at Battle Abbey as Bertuilay and members of the family held high offices in the county and the country and served as soldiers of the Crown. John Barttelot fought at Agincourt; another died while leading the Petworth Volunteers against the Boers; and his brother lost his life while searching for Dr Livingstone in Africa.

(G) Church of St Mary the Blessed Virgin, Stopham

Architectural features of this church point to an original building not later than the eleventh century. The chancel arch is Norman and on the outside of the north wall of the chancel is one of the original lancet windows. Embedded in the Sussex marble floor of the nave are brass effigies to twelve members of the Barttelot family. The octangular font is thirteenth century and the regimental colours of the 1st Battalion of the Coldstream Guards hang on the north wall above memorials to two members of the Barttelot family who served with that regiment. Thomas Newcombe preached here for more than sixty years and in the churchyard is the grave of Arthur Gilligan (1894-1976), one of the county's most distinguished cricketers.

WALK 7 – CISSBURY RING

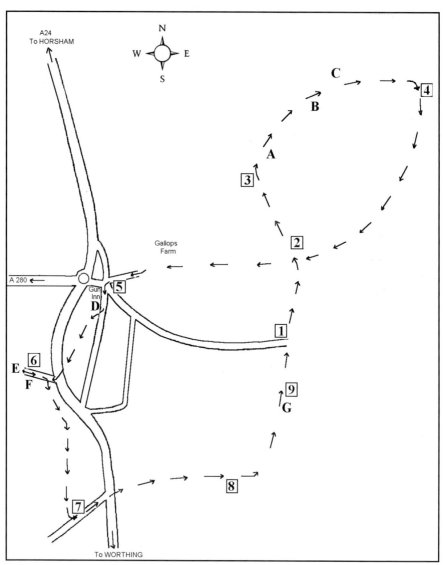

A – SOUTH DOWNS WAY. **B** – DEW POND. **C** – CHANCTONBURY HILL. **D** – GUN INN.
E – FINDON PLACE. **F**–ST JOHN'S CHURCH. **G** – CISSBURY RING.

The Gun Inn at Findon.

Walk 7 – Cissbury Ring

This walk offers the opportunity to split the full circuit into two shorter walks or retain the full walk. The walk out to Chanctonbury Ring provides splendid views back over Cissbury Ring while the walk to Findon shows how close the world of today has encroached on this ancient hill-fort. Passing the Gun Inn in the heart of the village the route crosses the A24 to visit Findon Place in its peaceful setting next to St John's church, before making the ascent to Cissbury Ring and the conclusion of this walk.

INFORMATION BOARD	
ACCESS/PARKING:	At Cissbury Ring, approached by well signposted road from Findon, off the A24 north of Worthing.
MAP REFERENCE:	Landranger 198, grid reference 139085
DISTANCE:	Full walk 8.75 miles (14km), Chanctonbury Ring 5.25 miles (8.5km), Findon 5 miles (8km)
TIME TO ALLOW:	Full Walk: 4 hrs. Chanctonbury Ring: 2.5 hrs. Findon: 2.5 hrs
TERRAIN:	Downland tracks, across fields and metalled road. Steady ascents to Chanctonbury Ring and Cissbury Ring. Parts may be muddy after wet weather
TOILETS/REFRESHMENTS:	Gun Inn, Findon
ROUTE:	Cissbury Ring–South Downs Way–Chanctonbury Ring–Findon Place and church–Roger's Farm–Cissbury Ring.

Directions:

1 From the car park proceed away from Cissbury Ring as far as the wide cross-tracks, from where there is a good view back. Turn left here then in 100 yards (95m) right, along a track which may be muddy after rain.

2 Pass New Cottages and in 200m yards (190m) turn right through gate, heading diagonally left across the field to a gate onto the road. Cross straight over the road and continue diagonally left again, keeping ahead up a dirt track.

3 As the track levels out, turn right at the cross-tracks to begin a steady climb up to meet the **South Downs Way (A).** Continue ahead past the **dew pond (B)** to **Chanctonbury Ring (C).**

4 Turn right at the next cross-tracks and return to the wide cross-tracks (see **1**). To return to the car park keep straight ahead. To continue to Findon turn right, keeping ahead to the T-junction by the entrance to Gallops Farm. Turn left here.

5 Turn left at the **Gun Inn (D)** along the High Street, then right beside the Village Hall. Go through the kissing gate and across the next field to the road. Cross the busy A24 and keep ahead down the road to **Findon Place (E)** and **St John's church (F).**

6 Retrace steps, turning right through the metal kissing gate by public footpath signpost. At South Lodge turn left and at the T-junction turn right. Follow the track round to the left at Stable Cottage.

7 Turn left at the road by a small car park, cross the A24 and continue along the public bridleway. Where the path splits, fork right, and pass through the gate before bearing right uphill towards Cissbury Ring. Head for the gap in the hedge about 50 yards (45m) below the perimeter fencing.

8 Pass through the metal gate and along an obvious track as far as the multi-armed signpost by the National Trust sign. Turn left here through the South Gate of **Cissbury Ring (G)** following the wide track ahead. Gorse surrounds the trig point at the summit, from where there are spectacular views all around.

9 Head inland a little to the left of the trig point to where there are steps leading down to the car park.

POINTS OF INTEREST

(A) South Downs Way

This was one of six long-distance footpaths recommended by a special committee on Footpaths and Access to the Countryside in 1947. It was originally intended that the route should run from Eastbourne to Winchester, where it would join the Pilgrims Way, and continue to a point west of Salisbury. Fifteen years later the National Parks Commission, the predecessor to the Countryside Commission, put forward a revised route and this received ministerial approval the following year.

On 15 July 1972 the South Downs Way, stretching from Eastbourne to the West Sussex county boundary near Buriton, was officially opened by Lord Shawcross. The Way is by no means a new route, for the greater part of it was already in existence even when the special committee deliberated back in 1947, for much of it is ancient trackway that has now been made accessible to man and horse along its entirety. Waymarkers of various kinds direct the user, in some instances merely by the use of an acorn sign, the Commission's long distance route symbol.

(B) Dew pond

A dew pond is an artificial clay pond which holds rain water and used by shepherds and farmers to water their stock. They were often built in chalk and limestone areas and the oldest of them date back to the seventeenth century, although they were still being made in the 1940s. Their builders often worked at night, digging the symmetrical hollows before lining them with puddled clay. Good ones retain their water even in the driest of weather, for the true art was in the positioning of the pond to collect the maximum amount of rainwater running off the land and permitting as little evaporation as possible.

(C) Chanctonbury Hill

This famous clump of beech trees, decimated in the 1987 hurricane, was planted in 1760 by the young Charles Goring of Wiston House. It is said he climbed the hill daily with bottles of water to aid their early growth and he lived to see them reach maturity, for he was ninety when he died. The

71

Chanctonbury Ring – after its devastation by the 1987 hurricane.

landmark is visible more than 60km away and in the centre of the ring is the site of a square Romano-British temple in which coins and pottery were found dating back to the first century AD.

(D) Gun Inn

Part of this inn was a gunsmith's shop in 1722, hence its name. By the nineteenth century the village had become a centre for the training of racehorses and Kermit, winner of the 1867 Derby, was stabled at the Gun for the innkeeper, William Goater, trained the horse and his cousin, Ian Goater, rode it to victory at Epsom.

(E) Findon Place

A handsome Georgian house with parts possibly dating back to the sixteenth century. Today it is privately owned and not open to the public.

(F) St John's Church

The known history of the church goes back to 1053 when, according to a contract which has been preserved, it was supplied with timber. The lower part of the tower is probably Saxon, and the rest of it may be Norman, but only the arch above the south transept door can definitely be attributed to Norman craftsmen. The distinctive feature of the church is its timber roof, which covers nave and aisle in a single span and which may well be more than 500 years old. The oak screen dates from around 1300 and the Purbeck marble font was added when the church was restored in 1867.

(G) Cissbury Ring

This extensive hill fort dates from the late Iron Age, about 250 BC, although there are traces of the shafts of flint mines sunk by men of the Bronze and New Stone Age in the surrounding area. A triangulation pillar stands at the Ring's summit, 602 feet above sea level, and on a clear day it is possible to see Beachy Head in the east and the Isle of Wight in the west. Although it bears no trace of siege or even military occupation, the vast and elaborate scale of Cissbury Ring shows that it was of great importance to the people who built it as a place of protection for themselves and their possessions in times of danger. The ditch surrounding the ramparts, built between 400 and 250 BC, is almost 1.25 miles (2km) in circumference and encloses an area of about 82 acres. The ramparts, which continued to be fortified until 50 BC, still rise to 20ft and are most prominent at the eastern and southern gateways. Outside the main rampart was another, lower bank, which can still be seen, and beyond that was the ditch that formed the hill fort's outer line of defence.

During the latter part of the Roman occupation, the site was re-fortified and the height of the original timber and chalk ramparts raised by a turf wall. The hill fort was known simply as Bury – the stronghold – and only after the Saxon chief, Aelle, gave Chichester to his son, Cissa, in 477 AD did it begin to take its present day prefix. Today it is under the protection of the National Trust.

WALK 8 – BRAMBER

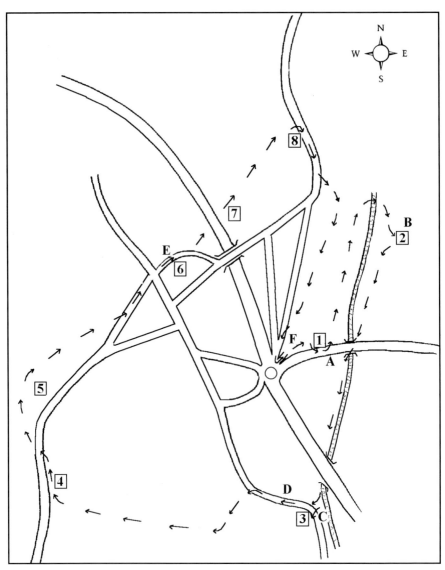

A – ST MARY'S HOUSE. **B** – BEEDING CHURCH. **C** – ST BOTOLPH'S CHURCH.
D – ANNINGTON. **E** – STEYNING. **F** – BRAMBER CASTLE.

St Botolph's church, showing the bricked-up arches where an extra aisle was added in 1560.

Walk 8 – Bramber

Bramber is a regular winner of the Sussex in Bloom competition each year, and it also has the remains of a castle, an interesting church and one of the finest timber-framed medieval houses in Sussex. This walk also visits Beeding church and the site of Sele Priory before following the course of the River Adur to join the South Downs Way on through Annington to the top of the Downs where the views are breathtaking. It then descends to Steyning, where St Cuthman came with his mother in a wheelbarrow, before returning to Bramber to visit the castle site and the church.

INFORMATION BOARD	
ACCESS/PARKING:	Car park opposite the Castle Hotel, Bramber
MAP REFERENCE:	Landranger 198, grid reference 188106
DISTANCE:	8 miles (12.8km)
TIME TO ALLOW:	4 hours
TERRAIN:	Well-defined paths across fields, well-used riverside paths, the South Downs Way and slabbed pavement. The route at point **3** requires a steady climb up the South Downs Way and at point **5** a steepish descent into Steyning. Neither are too arduous.
TOILETS/REFRESHMENTS:	White Horse Inn, Steyning (or other venues in the village off the route) or the Castle Hotel, Bramber. Toilets also at Bramber car park
ROUTE:	Bramber–St Mary's House–Beeding church–River Adur–Botolphs–South Downs Way–Annington–Steyning Bowl–Round Hill–Steyning–Bramber Castle–Bramber church, Bramber.

St Mary's House, Bramber.

Directions

1 Turn left out of the car park, passing **St Mary's House (A)** on the right, then turn left at the public footpath signpost and follow the well-defined path to a footbridge. Cross the river and turn right along the riverbank, before turning off left opposite the church, across the bridge and up some steps to **Beeding church (B)**, next door to which was Sele Priory.

2 Retrace steps, as if returning to the riverbank, and turn left at the public footpath signpost and follow the path through to small caravan park. Turn left along the riverbank to bridge and cross the river before turning left along the opposite bank and under the A283 as far as T-junction. Turn right here on to the South Downs Way and **St Botolph's church (C)**.

3 Return to the South Downs Way and follow it through to **Annington (D)**, turning left at the Way signpost. Continue through a wooden gate. On the right is Bramber Beeches, an enclosure planted by the West Sussex Federation of Women's Institutes to mark its Diamond Jubilee in 1979.

4 Follow the South Downs Way right beside the road at the head of Steyning Bowl, past the hang gliders' car park, before crossing the road and continuing to a memorial stone to Walter Langmead, a Sussex farmer.

5 Take the public bridleway, signposted Steyning 1.5 miles, and turn off right at the five-path junction. At the T-junction overlooking Steyning Round Hill bear right. Take the left fork at the public bridleway signpost, and continue along the metalled road into **Steyning (E)**.

6 Cross straight over into Church Street by the White Horse Inn to St Andrews church. Keep straight ahead at the end of the churchyard then turn left alongside the wooden fence on the right at the public footpath signpost. Keep ahead through the small housing estate to the bypass, which cross with care.

7 Down the steps and across the stile before keeping to the footpath alongside the fence. At the metalled road by the small sub-station turn right. It soon emerges into a dust track.

8 At the T-junction turn right, and as the road swings round right at the Downs Link signpost, bear left to cross the stile and head back across the field towards the bridge. Turn right in 200 yards (190m) at the public footpath signpost, then left at the road and left again at the towers of **Bramber Castle (F)**. Visit Bramber church before continuing down the steps and back to the car park.

POINTS OF INTEREST

(A) St Mary's House
This Grade I listed medieval house was built on earlier twelfth century Knights Templar foundations around 1470 and is one of the best examples of late fifteenth century timber-framing in Sussex. Its fine panelled rooms include a Tudor 'Painted Room', said to have been prepared for a visit by Queen Elizabeth I, which did not take place because of the bad state of the Sussex roads.

On the site of the car park once stood part of an 170ft long, 17ft wide stone bridge across the Adur. It had four arches and a large chapel above the centre pier on the south side. After the Dissolution, St Mary's House became the property of the Crown and then passed into private ownership. It was extensively restored by later owners and today has charming gardens with amusing topiary and holds a Tourist Board commendation.

St Peter's church, Upper Beeding.

(B) Beeding church

Officially the church is in Upper Beeding, sited geographically lower than Lower Beeding, which is four miles from Horsham. St Peter's was the priory church belonging to Sele Priory, a Benedictine monastery founded by William de Braose, who also built Bramber castle. Sele reverted to the Crown after the Dissolution and was annexed to Magdalen College, Oxford, which unfortunately holds no deeds or documents relating to it. One record does exist, however, and that refers to a visit by the Bishop of Dover in July 1538. On his arrival he 'found neither friar nor secular, but the doors open; there was none to serve God and had not been for some time'. The only connection with Sele Priory visible today is the tiny doorway said to have been used by the friars.

(C) St Botolph's church

A Roman bridge spanned the river near here carrying one of the earliest trade routes in Britain – the tin route from Cornwall – and a flourishing community lived hereabouts. The present church stands on the foundations of an eighth century church known as St Peter's-by-the-Bridge. Changing tides resulted in the destruction of the bridge and many of the buildings by flooding and by Tudor times the village had lost its prosperity and most of its population. Large parts of the church, as seen today, are of the original Saxon construction, particularly the south wall of the nave and the chancel arch and wall. The original north wall was removed around 1250 when an aisle was added to cater for the growing population and it was around this time when its dedication to St Peter was changed and it became known as St Botolph's. When the population declined the new aisle was demolished but the now bricked-up arches which led to it can be seen on both the inside and outside of the north wall. Traces of wall paintings are also still visible on the chancel arch. A fourteenth century Priest's House still stands beside the church, albeit much altered and enlarged today.

(D) Annington
The Annigas, or Anna's people, settled on a dun or hill here and the place was recorded as Anningadun in AD956. The Manor of Aningatune was recorded in *Domesday Survey* as a busy agricultural area and in 1428 it was referred to as *Vetere Ponte* or the old bridge, a name by which the area was known as long ago as 1296. Today Annington manor house still stands on the hill although there is little else here of its once illustrious past.

(E) Steyning
The first mention of Steyning was around AD 880 and it was listed in *Domesday* as Staninges, becoming known as Steyninge in 1316. It was a port in Saxon times when the estuary of the Adur stretched further inland, and its patron saint is St Cuthman who founded the first church here in the ninth century. Legend has it that Cuthman, a destitute shepherd boy, was obliged to push his sick mother around in a wheeled box he had made for her as they begged for food. They left their native Devon and trundled across country until they reached Steyning, where the cart collapsed. This was where their wanderings were meant to end, thought Cuthman, and he built a hut to shelter his mother and began single-handed to cut down trees to make a church in gratitude for God's help on their journey.

With the work almost done, one of the pillars suddenly buckled under the weight of the roof and Cuthman became alarmed in case the church might collapse. Then he saw a traveller by the door who appeared to be perturbed by his concern.

'O man of little faith', said the stranger. 'To those who fear God nothing is impossible. Stretch forth thy hand and we will straighten it'.

Immediately, according to the legend, the pillar came upright and the stranger made himself known to Cuthman.

'I am Jesus, to whom thou buildest this house,' he said, and vanished.

When Cuthman died he was laid to rest on the site of his endeavour and the present church, surprisingly dedicated to St Andrew and not to him, was built on the same site. It appears deceptively small from the outside but its interior is vast. Its mighty arch, 38ft high, is one of the finest Norman structures in Britain and its nave has four magnificent arches leading up to it. King Ethulwulf, father of Alfred the Great, is buried in the church, and the slab with a double incised cross standing in the porch may have once covered his grave.

There is a small museum opposite the church, depicting the history of Steyning from its days as a port. One fifteenth century house, now Brotherhood Hall, became a grammar school just before the death of Shakespeare. Its star pupil, John Pell, is quoted in every school in the land, for it was he who gave the world the division symbol in mathematics.

(F) Bramber Castle

The castle that succeeded a fort is now in ruins, impressive as they are, with the surviving fragment of the keep 76ft high. It was built soon after the Norman Conquest by William de Braose and remained in his family until 1326 when it passed to Alice de Bohun and then to her eldest son, John de Mowbry. It had an uneventful history, being in use well into the fourteenth century, but although it is rumoured Cromwell's troops were responsible for its ruinous condition, in point of fact it was derelict long before the Civil War and never saw action, save for being held briefly in 1217 by William of Durston for King Louis of France. The castle was eventually owned by the Dukes of Norfolk who sold it in 1925 when it was acquired by the National Trust for the nation.